ROCKETS

Written by
Betsy Buttonwood

Illustrated by
Donald Crews

GoodYearBooks

In the red rocket is . . .

a blue rocket.
In the blue rocket is . . .

a purple rocket.
In the purple rocket is . . .

a pink rocket.
In the pink rocket is . . .

a gray rocket.

In the gray rocket is . . .

a yellow rocket.
In the yellow rocket is . . .

a little brown mouse!